I am PERFECTLY ME

AFFIRMATIONS FROM A TO Z

WRITTEN BY MARSHA MEADOWS

ILLUSTRATED BY COURTNEY MONDAY

Manufactured in the United States of America

Cataloging-in-Publication data for this book is available from the Library of Congress

ISBN: 978-1-7363274-0-1

FIRST EDITION –

Illustrations: Courtney Monday

Editing: WesCourt Advisors

USA $15.99

DEDICATION

To my sons Willie "3" & Wesley and my nephew Micah, you are amazing boys who inspire, encourage, and motivate me every day. Your energy, love, and hugs light up my world. I Love You. This book is also dedicated to my goddaughters Destiny, Autumn, Ryleigh, Georgia, Faith & Kyia, and all of my little cousins, I can't wait to see how you influence the world. Keep being Incredibly You!!!

ACKNOWLEDGEMENTS

Thank you to Jyneisha Washington for your input and encouragement. Courtney Monday, your illustrations are outstanding and bring the affirmations to life. To Dr. Adair White-Johnson, thank you and your team for helping me pull this book together. To my mother, father, brother, family & friends (Monique & Tamika), who listened to and supported me, thank you.

5

I am **awesome** and **amazing**. I **always** do my best!

I am **brave** and **brilliant.**
I **believe** in me!

I am **creative**, **confident** and **courageous**. I **can** **change** the world.

I am a **dreamer!**
I **dare** to be **different.**

I am **equal** to **everyone.**
I am **exceptional** and full of **energy.**
I am **everything** I desire to be.

I am **funny** and **friendly.**
I am **free** to be me.

11

I am **giving,**
grateful and **great.**
I **get** what I **give!**

I am **happy**, **healthy** and **helpful**.

I am intelligent, important and full of imagination.

I am incredibly me!

14

I am joyful.

I am kind.

I am **loving** and **loved.**
I **love** to **learn.**
I am a **leader!!!**

I am **my** best when I'm being **me.**
I **matter** and I **make** a difference.

I am **nice** to others and
I am **needed** in this world.

I **never** give up!

I am **one** with **others.**

There is **only one** me!
I am **outstanding!**

I am **powerful,**
protected and **proud.**
I have a **purpose.**

I am **quirky** and
have amazing **qualities.**

I am **royalty.**

I am **respectful** and **radiant.**

I am **strong** and **smart**.
I am **super!**

I am **teachable** and **thankful**.
I tell the **truth**.

I am unique and unafraid.

I am **valued** and **very** special.

I am **wise** and **worthy**. I am a **winner!**

I am e**X**traordinary!

I am **young.**
I am **zealous.**

I can.
I will.
I AM...
PERFECTLY ME!

Made in the USA
Columbia, SC
13 January 2021